Influence In Action™

Gains Proven Results And Drives Sales

Written by

Robert J. Smith, MFA

Foreword by

Forbes Riley

INFLUENCE IN ACTION™
GAINS PROVEN RESULTS AND DRIVES SALES

Copyright

No part of this book may be reproduced or transmitted in any form or by any means, electronic or mechanical, including photocopying, recording or by any information storage and retrieval system, without written permission from the authors, except for the inclusion of brief quotations in a review.

Limit of Liability Disclaimer: The information provided in this book is for informational purposes only and is not intended to be a source of direct consulting with respect to the material presented. The information and/or documents contained in this book do not constitute legal or financial advice and should never be used without first consulting a qualified advisor to determine which strategies may best fit your individual needs and be customized to your unique situation.

The publisher and the authors do not make any guarantee or other promise as to any results that may be obtained from using the

INFLUENCE IN ACTION™
GAINS PROVEN RESULTS AND DRIVES SALES

content in this book. Meeting with a qualified advisor and conducting your own research and due diligence is always recommended. To the maximum extent permitted by law, the publisher and the authors disclaim any and all liability in the event any information, commentary, analysis, opinions, advice and/or recommendations contained in this book prove to be inaccurate, incomplete, unreliable, or result in any type of loss.

Content contained or made available through this book is not intended to constitute legal advice or financial advice, and no attorney-client relationship is formed through this published work.

Client relationships may only be formed at:

https://SmithProfits.com/Services

A no charge, no obligation initial consultation may be obtained at:

https://SmithProfits.com/Contact/

INFLUENCE IN ACTION™
GAINS PROVEN RESULTS AND DRIVES SALES

Earnings Disclaimer: All income examples in this book are examples. They are not intended to represent or guarantee that everyone will achieve the same results. It is understood that each individual's success will be determined by his or her desire, dedication, background, effort, and motivation to work. There is no guarantee the reader will duplicate any of the results stated here. The reader recognizes that any and all business endeavors have inherent risk of loss of capital.

No Agency Relationship: The opinions of each co-author do not necessarily constitute the opinions of Robert J. Smith, Robert J. Smith Productions, or Smith Profits. Co-author content does not in any way constitute an agency relationship between any co-author and of Robert J. Smith, Robert J. Smith Productions, or Smith Profits.

INFLUENCE IN ACTION™
GAINS PROVEN RESULTS AND DRIVES SALES

Influence in Action™ Gains Proven Results and Drives Sales

1st Edition. 2024

ASIN: (Amazon Kindle)

ISBN: 978-1-965538-02-9

TRADEMARKS: All product names, logos, and brands are the property of their respective owners. All company, product, and service names used in this book are for identification purposes only. Using these names, logos, and brands does not imply endorsement. All other trademarks cited herein are the property of their respective owners.

INFLUENCE IN ACTION™
GAINS PROVEN RESULTS AND DRIVES SALES

INFLUENCE IN ACTION™ has a Trademark pending International Class 016: Series of printed non-fiction books in the field of BUSINESS.

Copyright © 2024, **Robert J. Smith, MFA.** All rights reserved.

Book Layout © 2024, **Published by:** RJS Pro Publishing and The Publishing Genie.

INFLUENCE IN ACTION™
GAINS PROVEN RESULTS AND DRIVES SALES

Table of Contents

Dedication 10

Acknowledgements 11

Foreword 13

Prologue 18

Chapter One 23

   Always Stay True to Your Word 23

Chapter Two 28

   Stand on the Shoulders of Giants.............. 28

Chapter Three 35

   Factual Storytelling™ 35

Chapter Four 49

   Positioning – Why Rankings Matter 49

Chapter Five 55

   Authority Marketing 55

Chapter Six 59

   Scarcity Marketing 59

Chapter Seven 65

   Marketing with Consistency and Selling through Commitment 65

Chapter Eight 70
Smile 70
Chapter Nine 81
Customer/Client Conformity and Referrals 81
Chapter Ten 84
Marketing through Affiliation 84
Chapter Eleven 87
Playing the Percentages 87
Epilogue 92
About The Author 96
Coming Soon 102
Coming Soon from *SMITH COMICS:* 108

INFLUENCE IN ACTION™
GAINS PROVEN RESULTS AND DRIVES SALES

"There is no greater harm than that of time wasted." – Michelangelo

Outside forces caused much time to be wasted in the launching of this book. Due to this fact, no one understands the words of one of the greatest artists in the history of the world more than I do.

Therefore, Wise Reader, this book is dedicated to you and to everyone who understands the importance of time and the obligation that each of us has to humanity and to ourselves to refuse to waste it.

INFLUENCE IN ACTION™
GAINS PROVEN RESULTS AND DRIVES SALES

Dedication

This book is dedicated to my mother, Paulette who never hesitates to take *ACTION!*

And, to every reader who never hesitates to take *ACTION!*

INFLUENCE IN ACTION™
GAINS PROVEN RESULTS AND DRIVES SALES

Acknowledgements

This book would not have been possible without:

Encouragement from my amazing mother, Paulette, for whom I am thankful for attending my Creative Writing Master of Fine Arts commencement ceremony and being prouder than I could have expected when I was named Valedictorian.

My dearly departed father, Robert, whom I wish were still here. I'll be forever grateful to him for teaching me to always keep my word and for many other life lessons as well.

My good brother Ron, whose All Smiles Guarantee inspired *MY SMILE, YOU'RE ON BRANDED CAMERA* article in Forbes, which was the catalyst for this book.

My wonderful children; Ashley, Austin, and Sabrina who have all inspired me with their influence and leadership in sports, coaching middle school and high school sports teams, and in their professions, as well as with all of their published works.

My beautiful girlfriend of seventeen years and counting, Sharon, whose patience I appreciated while I worked nights and weekends on this book. I very much appreciate her fine editing skills as well.

And finally, my dear departed friend, Nani, an author who always kept her word.

With My Mother, Paulette, and My Brother, Ron at a Detroit Tigers Spring Training Game

INFLUENCE IN ACTION™
GAINS PROVEN RESULTS AND DRIVES SALES

Foreword

As I sit down to pen this foreword, I'm reminded of the countless moments in my career where influence was not just a tool but a transformative force. I am Forbes Riley, often referred to as the Queen of Pitch. My journey from being an actress and TV host to becoming an internationally recognized motivational speaker, fitness expert, and business coach has been nothing short of extraordinary. I've had the privilege of working with some of the most influential figures in the industry, including the legendary Billy Mays, with whom I co-created some of the most successful infomercials in history.

Throughout my career, I've learned that influence is an art and a science. It's about connecting with people on a deeper level, understanding their needs, and delivering a message that resonates and inspires action. From launching the SpinGym, a product that has changed the fitness landscape, to helping entrepreneurs perfect their pitches, influence has been at the heart of everything I do.

One of my proudest accomplishments is the community I've built around the power of the pitch. Whether it's through my pitch bootcamps, keynote speeches, or my Inner Circle membership, I've had the honor of guiding thousands towards achieving their dreams. My philosophy is simple: to influence effectively, one must be authentic, passionate, and relentless in their pursuit of excellence.

This book, "Influence in Action™," is a testament to the power of influence in our lives. It encapsulates the principles and strategies that can turn ordinary individuals into extraordinary influencers. The pages ahead are filled with insights and actionable advice that will empower you to harness your own influence and make a meaningful impact in your personal and professional life.

For entrepreneurs, mastering influence can mean the difference between success and failure. It's the ability to pitch your ideas convincingly, attract investors, and build a loyal customer base. Influence enables you to create a compelling brand story, foster partnerships, and navigate the challenges of the business world with confidence and finesse.

For leaders, influence is the key to inspiring and motivating your team. It's about leading by example, communicating your vision effectively, and fostering a culture of trust and collaboration. Influence helps you to bring out the best in others, driving innovation and achieving remarkable results.

For individuals in any walk of life, influence allows you to build stronger relationships, advocate for your needs, and create opportunities for growth and advancement. It's about being a positive force in your community, making a difference, and leaving a lasting legacy.

As you embark on this journey, remember that influence is not about manipulating others to get what you want. It's about creating a win-win situation where both

INFLUENCE IN ACTION™
GAINS PROVEN RESULTS AND DRIVES SALES

parties benefit. It's about building trust, fostering relationships, and delivering value. When you master the art of influence, you become a catalyst for change, inspiring others to see the world through a lens of possibility and potential.

I am thrilled to see how "Influence in Action™" will equip you with the tools and mindset to become a force of positive change. Whether you're an entrepreneur, a leader, or someone who simply wants to make a difference, this book will be your guide to mastering the art of influence.

INFLUENCE IN ACTION™
GAINS PROVEN RESULTS AND DRIVES SALES

Here's to your journey of becoming an influential force in action.

With gratitude and excitement,

Dr. Forbes Riley,

The Queen of Perfect Pitch

www.ForbesRiley.com

Forbes Riley and Her SpinGym, Before My Fighter Jet Flight for *UNDERSIZE ME*©

INFLUENCE IN ACTION™
GAINS PROVEN RESULTS AND DRIVES SALES

Prologue

Forbes is right when she says, "Whether you're an entrepreneur, a leader, or someone who simply wants to make a difference, this book will be your guide to mastering the art of influence."

As a home market merchandiser for Coca-Cola USA, I was able to positively influence my store owners and managers as well as their customers to outsell everyone else and develop the #1 sales route in the territory.

This was accomplished through service with a smile, always delivering my product on or ahead of schedule, and always taking the time to stop for "A Coke and a Smile" with anyone who asked. I wasn't just a Coke Man, I was *their* Coke Man.

INFLUENCE IN ACTION™
GAINS PROVEN RESULTS AND DRIVES SALES

Next to My Coca-Cola Delivery Truck, Circa 1985

It was the same in financial services. My clients all knew that while I represented many of the largest companies in the world, I always placed their interests first. I wasn't just any financial services advisor; I was *their* financial services advisor. This led to sales and achievement records at John Hancock, New York Life, and BankAtlantic which ultimately merged into BB&T which became Sun Trust and ultimately, Truist. I was also able to lead The Equitable Life Assurance Society, Mutual of New York (MONY), and AXA Financial in worldwide sales as well.

INFLUENCE IN ACTION™
GAINS PROVEN RESULTS AND DRIVES SALES

For the past two decades, I've been consulting with financial advisory firms and other companies, to aid them in achieving similar results. When asked to speak to groups, I'm often asked if I've written a book on the practical applications of influence and how anyone may ethically apply ethical persuasion to achieve success.

As my parents and grandparents have always said, "There is no time like the present."

When developing the concept for *INFLUENCE IN ACTION*™, I began with two premises that I expect will help you derive the most benefit so that you may *GAIN PROVEN RESULTS AND DRIVE SALES* with what you read here.

We must all have a bias toward *ACTION* to achieve optimal success.

INFLUENCE IN ACTION™
GAINS PROVEN RESULTS AND DRIVES SALES

With Sharon and My Youngest Daughter, Sabrina, Before Calling *"ACTION!"* In the film, *JET FIGHTER*©

As President Theodore Roosevelt said, "Get action! Do things; be sane; don't fritter away your time; create, act, take a place wherever you are and be somebody; get action!"

I've personally taken all of the actions recommended in this book and I've gained proven results with each and every one of them. It is my sincere belief that you, Wise Reader, may do the same. If and only if, you act*!*

INFLUENCE IN ACTION™
GAINS PROVEN RESULTS AND DRIVES SALES

As there are an estimated 160 million book titles worldwide, it is indeed an honor that you have chosen to read *INFLUENCE IN ACTION™ GAINS PROVEN RESULTS AND DRIVES SALES*.

It is my sincere hope that you will find value in what I have learned and found to be effective in the pursuit of achievement each and every day. It is also my sincere hope that you will achieve success, as all of my consulting clients have. Each and every one of them.

It's not enough to learn all of the principles necessary to gain more *influence* in order to become more effective at what we do. To improve present business results and to create the future we want, *we must act, and we must* act now*!*

INFLUENCE IN ACTION™
GAINS PROVEN RESULTS AND DRIVES SALES

Chapter One

Always Stay True to Your Word

Whenever we want to put *INFLUENCE IN ACTION*™ *TO GAIN PROVEN RESULTS AND DRIVE SALES,* we must always keep our word. We must do what we say we are going to do and we must lead by example.

"Work hard. Do your best. Keep your word." – Harry Truman

President Truman was the world leader largely credited with ending World War II and bringing more than 13.6 million Americans home, including my grandfather.

When you keep your word with people, you build trust with them. When you build trust with them, they are more apt to do business with you. It's as simple as that. Of course, trust is a two-way street. As important as it is to keep your word and be trustworthy, it is equally important to demand the same of everyone you do business with. This includes; customers, clients, strategic partners, vendors, employees and the like.

It is also important to understand human nature to be able to *influence* others and persuade them to take positive actions that are in their best interests. Again, it is equally important to recognize when others are trying to *unethically influence* you. There is never a good reason to work with strategic partners, vendors, clients, customers, or anyone who fails to honor his or her commitments or to be consistent in his or her words and *actions*.

Good business is always a two-way street. While there is never any harm in doing a good deed for someone who fails to reciprocate in kind, it never makes sense to continue to give to those who demand more than they are allotted, more than they are entitled to, or more than they deserve. That's just bad business.

INFLUENCE IN ACTION™
GAINS PROVEN RESULTS AND DRIVES SALES

This is what makes understanding the Principles of Ethics so powerful. Once you understand them, not only do you obtain the ability to understand human nature so that you may predictably run your business, improve your marketing and increase your sales, you can also recognize unethical behaviors and negative *influences* so that you are able to avoid making bad business decisions that produce negative outcomes.

When a situation such as this arises, a person with character has three choices:

1. Allow the lack of ethics of others to sway you into abandoning your ethics.
2. Allow the negative actions of others to lull you into an unproductive state of inaction.
3. Do what all successful people do, *TAKE ACTION* to correct the situation.

To take immediate, corrective *ACTION* is always the most productive route to take.

INFLUENCE IN ACTION™
GAINS PROVEN RESULTS AND DRIVES SALES

Always keep your word and surround yourself with others who always keep their word as well when you do, you will *GAIN* more *PROVEN* and positive *RESULTS* and *DRIVE* more *RESULTS* than you ever thought possible.

Within weeks of completing my Master of Fine Arts degree as Valedictorian at Full Sail University and my Feature Film Writing Certificate "With Distinction" simultaneously at UCLA, I asked all of my fellow graduates to take *ACTION* and join me in Hollywood "Pitch Fest." None of my peers acted. While they are still all working their day jobs, I've been fortunate enough to earn hundreds of writing, acting, directing, producing, and other credits in the Internet Movie Database (IMDb). The bonus benefit is always TOP of Google search rankings.

INFLUENCE IN ACTION™
GAINS PROVEN RESULTS AND DRIVES SALES

**With Sharon at Warner Brothers Studios
After Pitching Feature-Length Screenplays**

In order to create the results that you want, *you must TAKE ACTION!*

INFLUENCE IN ACTION™ *GAINS PROVEN RESULTS* provides you with all of the tools, methods, guidance, and assistance that you need to succeed. The decision to act is up to you.

INFLUENCE IN ACTION™
GAINS PROVEN RESULTS AND DRIVES SALES

Chapter Two

Stand on the Shoulders of Giants

In a 1675, letter to Robert Hooke, Sir Isaac Newton wrote "If I have seen further it is by standing on the shoulders of Giants." This is something I was fortunate to learn as a youngster and it has served me well.

I was also fortunate to attend Edison Elementary which gave me a deep appreciation for one the world's most prolific inventors, a man who brought us out of the darkness. I then attended Whittier Junior High, named for the poet quoted in my chapter, Playing the Percentages. Then, onto Franklin High. Reading the autobiography of Benjamin Franklin, *Poor Richard's Almanacks* and numerous books written about one of America's Founding Fathers also served me well. This all provided me with a voracious appetite for reading books by and about great American business leaders and my biggest interest, sports.

It was great to learn pitching from Detroit Tigers great, Denny McClain and hitting from "Mr. Tiger," Al Kaline as well as another childhood hero, Willie Horton. I was fortunate to meet all of these giants later in life. When I was on the field for batting practice in Spring Training, Mr. Kaline tapped me on the shoulder. I turned around to face him and he said, "I've heard a lot about you, and I've been looking forward to meeting you." I was speechless.

INFLUENCE IN ACTION™
GAINS PROVEN RESULTS AND DRIVES SALES

Sharon and Mr. Tiger, Al Kaline

I was also fortunate enough to learn about hockey by reading about another childhood hero, Gordie Howe. Meeting "Mr. Hockey" was like meeting a real-life Superman. My girlfriend, Sharon Roznowski, and I met Mr. Howe by chance at Metro Airport. Ever since that meeting, whenever we are having a spectacular day, we refer to it as a Gordie Howe Day!

Before the Gordie Howe Days arrived, there was much work to be done. First, I was able to lean on the work ethic I learned from my parents and grandparents. That, along with the competitive drive I gained from winning multiple baseball championships, allowed me to build the #1 producing home market merchandiser route at Coca-Cola.

Sports teach discipline. They teach us how to compete and how to work as team players. We are always competing with our teammates and never against them. Sports teach us leadership. My children, Ashley, Austin, and Sabrina, have all been leaders since a very young age. They all excelled in college and each of them now excel in their careers.

INFLUENCE IN ACTION™
GAINS PROVEN RESULTS AND DRIVES SALES

**Your Author with a Very Young
Ashley and Austin Smith**

As a young financial advisor, working advanced markets with The John Hancock Companies in metro Detroit, I struggled to book appointments with executives of the Big Three; Ford, Chrysler, and General Motors. The financial advisory business is already highly competitive. I made it even tougher on myself by working in high-end markets rather than with families and "Mom and Pop shops."

I reached out to my General Agent, Laurence Mohn, to see how I could better compete with older, more experienced advisors. His solution was simple. "Gain more authority." I immediately set out to do just that.

The trouble was that I didn't have 48-months to earn the Chartered Life Underwriter (CLU) and Chartered Financial Consultant (ChFC) professional designations from The American College. Instead, I completed both programs in just 13 months, turning out a company record. No one had ever come close to that speed from 1927 to 1992.

That record was not accomplished out of any need for recognition, it was earned out of necessity. With the desire to have children and start a family, the time to work and the time to succeed was now. When speaking with John Hancock media relations to do research for a

Forbes article last month, I discovered that record that still stands today.

https://www.forbes.com/councils/forbesbusinesscouncil/people/smittyrobertjsmith/

More importantly, the authority gained with those professional designations immediately helped me to book appointments and gain new clients. Better yet, those new clients followed my recommendations, and they gained financial security. They also referred their business associates, family, and friends to me.

I was able to reach the TOP 1% in worldwide production largely due to the Factual Storytelling™ methods that I had developed by reading books, attending lectures, and paying attention to what experienced and successful advisors were doing.

Chapter Three

Factual Storytelling™

Factual Storytelling™ is a giant step above everyday storytelling. While everyone knows that storytelling helps business owners and professionals to make sales, it's only with facts that we achieve the highest level of storytelling and we achieve optimal sales.

As we know, humans have been telling stories since we've been able to speak. This is how we communicate. People relate to stories on a visceral level. This is why stories are so effective as methods of influence and persuasion. This is also why stories are so effective for top salespeople. As humans, we make the majority of our buying decisions for emotional reasons, not for logical reasons.

In order to become a giant of a storyteller himself, Walt Disney stood on the shoulders of giants by retelling stories of; the Brothers Grimm (*The Valiant Little Tailor* and *Snow White*),

Perrault (*Cinderella* and *Sleeping Beauty*), Goethe (*The Sorcerer's Apprentice*), Collodi (*Pinocchio*), Andersen (*The Little Mermaid*), Carroll (*Alice in Wonderland*) and many others. Mr. Disney captivated audiences through stories and fairy tales as others did who came before him.

Sharon and I live right next door to Walt Disney World on land that was owned by The Walt Disney Company until just a few years ago. As a result, we often frequent the parks. Most often, we visit EPCOT (Experimental Prototype Community of Tomorrow) where a brief history of our world is narrated by Dame Judi Dench, in the attraction, Spaceship Earth. The name comes from a term coined by the late Buckminster Fuller who also created the geodesic dome, the structure that the attraction is housed in. This brief history of our Spaceship Earth is also a brief history of storytelling.

Upon entering Spaceship Earth, we board our "time machines" and prepare to travel back to the dawn of our very existence. In the first scene of our story, we see cavemen confronting a Mastodon. Dame Dench starts us off, "Here, in this hostile world, is where our story begins. We are alone, struggling to survive until we learn to communicate with one another. Now we can hunt as a team and survive together." As we travel from the hunt, we see primitive drawings. "It takes 15,000 years to come up with the next bright idea: recording our knowledge on cave walls. There was only one small problem, when we moved, the recorded knowledge stayed behind."

We travel forward in time and see an ancient Egyptian working with a pestle. "Now, let's move ahead to ancient Egypt, because something is about to happen here that will change the future forever. This unknown Egyptian pounding reeds flat is inventing papyrus—a sort of paper. Papyrus, in turn, creates better record keeping of plans, designs, and unfortunately taxes. But it also brings with it the dawn of great civilizations." Now, we can share our stories, no differently than we are doing here.

INFLUENCE IN ACTION™
GAINS PROVEN RESULTS AND DRIVES SALES

"At this point, each civilization has its own form of writing, which none of the others can understand. But the Phoenicians, who trade with all of them, have a solution. They create a simple, common alphabet, adaptable to most languages. Remember how easy it was to learn your ABC's? Thank the Phoenicians—they invented them." You'd be surprised at how many people we see wearing T-shirts that read "Thank the Phoenicians" each and every time we visit EPCOT.

As we continue to travel through time we see; the Greeks create schools and teach mathematics, Romans build roads, and the burning of the Great Library of Alexandria. We discover that there were copies of some of these books in the Middle East and that some of our stories and recorded knowledge are recovered.

As we proceed through time, we see European monks copying books by hand, much like we saw them do in 1970s Xerox commercials on television. From there, we see two animatronic characters hard at work. "In

1450, Gutenberg invents the movable type printing press. Now knowledge can travel as fast as these new books... and travel they do. Books make it easier to invent the future in every field, and the result is an incredible explosion of innovation that we call the Renaissance."

Writing a book may not make you a Renaissance man or woman. What it will do is help you gain business if you write non-fiction geared toward your ideal client and you fill that book with Factual Storytelling™. Writing a book will also provide you with authority in the eyes of your clients and prospects, much as professional designations do. The biggest benefit is that writing books takes much less time than completing college programs do.

While in our "time machines" we continue on past a sculptor, some musicians and an animatronic Michelangelo painting The Sistine Chapel while lying on his back, supported by scaffolding. As we move on, "Books, it seems, were just the beginning. Now communication technology races headlong into the future, and soon people all over the world are sharing life's most important moments faster than ever before."

Back in America in the 19th century, we see a worker in a newspaper plant. Something cool that no one ever seems to notice is that while the animatronic worker faces us, he is holding the folded paper upside down so that we can read "CIVIL WAR IS OVER!"

We then travel past the invention of the telegraph, the telephone switchboard, the cinema "running" a newsreel of Jesse Owens winning Olympic Gold in 1936, a radio newsroom, a family watching the televised moon landing in 1969, a room with massive 1970s computers and then "a garage in California" with a lone inventor creating the personal computer.

From here, EPCOT guests are able to create a futuristic cartoon of themselves enjoying life in the future.

You, Wise Reader can do even better than that. You can bring Factual Storytelling™ into your life, career, and business to enjoy greater success than you ever have before.

I'll close this book with a factual story very close to my heart. This story illustrates the gains we achieve when we understand human nature and the losses we suffer when we choose to ignore them.

Before that story in Chapter Eleven, here is a Factual Storytelling™ example of how any professional in any business may use any genre of storytelling to get facts across to consumers.

As long as we stay true to the facts, we may use any type of story to make our proven solutions to even the most complicated consumer and business problems, easily understood by them.

People don't buy the features and benefits of our products and services; they buy solutions to their problems. It is our job, just as it is yours, to provide the best solutions that will solve their problems.

INFLUENCE IN ACTION™
GAINS PROVEN RESULTS AND DRIVES SALES

Blending Facts with Superheroes for Massive Success

Factual Storytelling™ helped me earn *TOP 1% worldwide production rankings.* However, it wasn't until I created such a story on the spot, that I was able to make a very complex financial issue easily understood by people who very much needed to understand it. This was necessary for a couple with an estate tax problem that would have lowered the standard of living for their heirs, had we not solved it for them. With this solution to their problem, I was able to propel my financial advisory practice to a #1 worldwide production ranking with Mutual of New York (MONY), AXA Financial and The Equitable.

All of the largest and most well-known financial services companies in America compete for estate planning cases in the very same fashion. They put together a team of financial advisors, insurance agents, CPAs and attorneys. Then, they put together very long and very complex estate plans and proposals. More often than not, this strategy does nothing more than intimidate and confuse prospective clients. As we know, a confused mind always says "No." So, why then take this tact?

It makes more sense to take very complex issues such as this and make them easy for prospects and clients to understand. That's what I did with *THE ADVENTURES OF INSURANCEMAN*. Long before *INSURANCEMAN* became a persuasive marketing and sales piece in comic book form, he was merely a story. A story that came about when I saw that my clients were confused about the real financial liquidity issues their family faced with the Internal Revenue Service. Tough financial issues at a time when they were least likely to want to deal with them.

We sat down together with a couple of blank legal pads and pencils while I created the story of *INSURANCEMAN*. We wrote down some key facts, some notes and some numbers based on their financial situation. I even drew a few pictures to clarify a few points for them. About twenty-minutes in, the husband slammed his hands down on my desk and exclaimed, "I've finally got it! I understand! I've been wrestling with this for six months, and I finally understand it!" Shortly thereafter, his wife beamed a huge smile and proudly said, "I finally understand as well."

They fully understood that the best solution for them was to buy life insurance to handle their estate tax for pennies on the dollar. The only obstacles now, were finding the liquidity to handle the premiums, and getting an elderly couple qualified for life insurance coverage at affordable rates. The easy part was solving the liquidity issue. I asked them to draw me a picture of the new home they had just built for themselves on the island of Nantucket. They drew me a beautiful picture of their home underneath a large sun that they had drawn a smiley face on. Next, I asked them to draw straight lines on the side of their house from the grass to the rooftop. We agreed that this represented all of their ready cash and accounts that could be turned into cash. I asked two simple questions:

INFLUENCE IN ACTION™
GAINS PROVEN RESULTS AND DRIVES SALES

1. When you pay for everyday necessities, do you take dollars off the top or the from the bottom of your liquid assets? The answer, as expected, was "from the top."

2. As we take money from the top, and your pile of cash continues to refill through interest and earnings, will you ever need to spend down to your last dollar? This time, the answer was also as expected, "No. Of course, not."

Through a lot of hard work with the medical underwriters with several large companies, I was able to get them both qualified. That case alone was worth $110,000.00 in commissions.

It was then that I realized the real power of storytelling to help people understand and solve their financial problems. Since estate planning cases are a very small part of the financial advisory business, I created *THE ADVENTURES OF INSURANCEMAN* to help insurance and financial advisors help their prospects and clients reach a better

INFLUENCE IN ACTION™
GAINS PROVEN RESULTS AND DRIVES SALES

understanding of what life insurance and annuities can help them accomplish with college funding and retirement planning.

THE ADVENTURES OF INSURANCEMAN© is available for licensing to professionals for whom we customize the inside front and back covers as well as the outside back cover. We've never seen a sales and marketing piece anywhere close to being as effective in bringing prospects and clients into our offices who are pre-disposed to following our advice.

The one thing we didn't anticipate is how effective this persuasive piece is in bringing in referrals. Clients naturally let their friends and relatives read *INSURANCEMAN,* and they book appointments. It's also amazing to see how well appointments go when advisors send this marketing piece out to prospects in advance of their initial consultations.

INFLUENCE IN ACTION™
GAINS PROVEN RESULTS AND DRIVES SALES

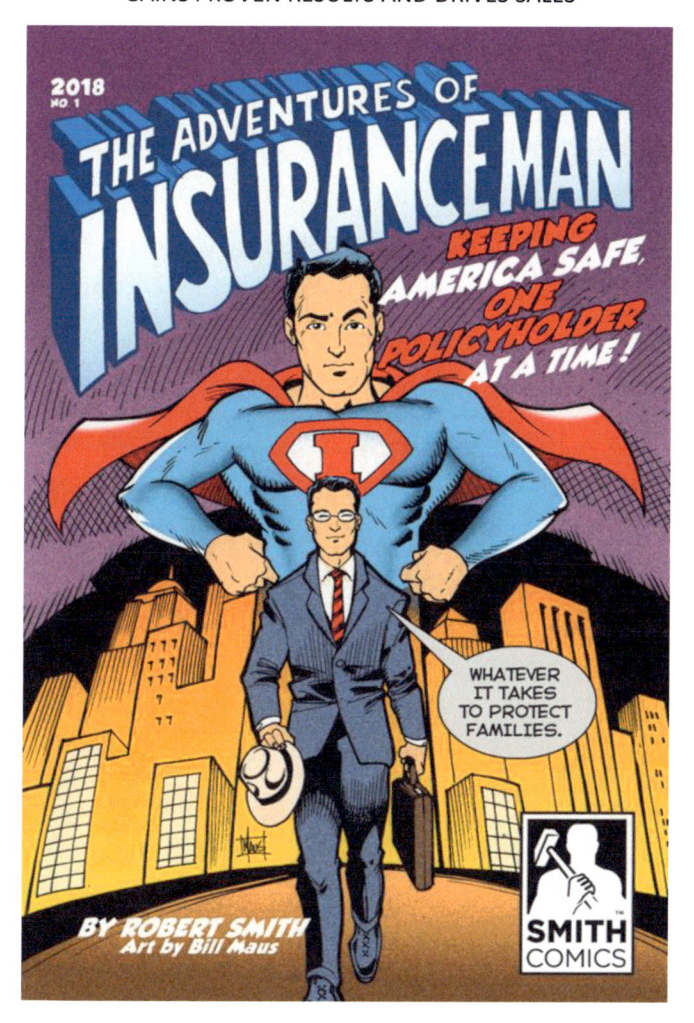

THE ADVENTURES OF INSURANCEMAN©
Pre-Sells Cases and Gains Referrals

INFLUENCE IN ACTION™
GAINS PROVEN RESULTS AND DRIVES SALES

One of the most amazing things I've seen is when I use *INSURANCEMAN* as a tool to help educate elementary school students in writing and public speaking when volunteering in Sharon's classroom. Their eyes light up and I can see them get excited about writing. When I come back weeks later, they eagerly show me comic books they have written. Some have even shown me song lyrics for me to read. It's impressive to see what kids can do, the very minute they upgrade their mindset to view their endless possibilities.

Chapter Four

Positioning – Why Rankings Matter

As I consult with clients on a daily basis, I often relate to them that I have stood on the shoulders of giants. I've read well over 200 books and worked with Fortune 500 Companies while in private practice for decades. This chapter highlights some of the most effective methods of all of that learning. It is your key to improved performance and results for you and your business. This is your roadmap to #1 worldwide rankings…provided that you put these proven methods to work for you, and you take <u>CONSISTENT ETHICAL ACTIONS IN ORDER TO SUCCEED WITH THEM</u>!

The best part about all of those decades of learning is that every strategy is based on logic and has been proven to succeed. Everything we do for our clients has been proven by ourselves and by others. Every strategy we employ is time-tested and proven to work.

INFLUENCE IN ACTION™
GAINS PROVEN RESULTS AND DRIVES SALES

These strategies are all based on decades of scientific research, testing, and measuring. Of course, an ethical approach is essential for the delivery of each and every recommendation.

Here is the key to your success as well as mine and everyone else's: Research and knowledge are essentially useless without application. All of the knowledge in the world is of no value without *ACTION*. This *ACTION* must be focused. Efficiencies and systems are paramount to optimal success. We benefit from quick wins just as our clients do. We start every client with easy to implement improvements that achieve massive results from day one.

I've been able to achieve individual success with these methods. E.g., #1 worldwide production rankings with The Equitable, MONY, and AXA Financial, and as part of a team with New York Life. I'm very pleased to have my name on a plaque on Madison Avenue alongside those of my teammates. These methods also work when in charge of teams. I've utilized them to gain #1 rankings with BankAtlantic which was merged into BB&T, SunTrust and ultimately,

Truist. As expected, these methods are not limited to financial services. I've used many of them to earn #1 sales ranking with Coca-Cola.

All of the proven business methods that I've learned over decades of experience coupled with what I've learned from decades of lectures and readings, have helped me to consistently rank in; *the TOP 1% in Financial Services, the TOP 1% in the Internet Movie Database (IMDb), and the TOP 1% in LinkedIn.* More importantly, these methods will help you do the same!

https://www.linkedin.com/in/RobertJSmithMFA/

We can help you improve your Social Selling Index (SSI) on LinkedIn. When you are ranked in the *TOP 1%* in your industry as well as the *TOP 1%* in your network, business flows to you much more easily.

INFLUENCE IN ACTION™
GAINS PROVEN RESULTS AND DRIVES SALES

These methods are unbeatable for your business and career as they will rank you on *the TOP of page one in Personal Name Brand Google Searches* and *the TOP of page one in Company Brand Name Google Searches*. It should be easier for you, as you likely won't have the same name as a Rock and Roll Hall of Famer, and NFL running back and other notables.

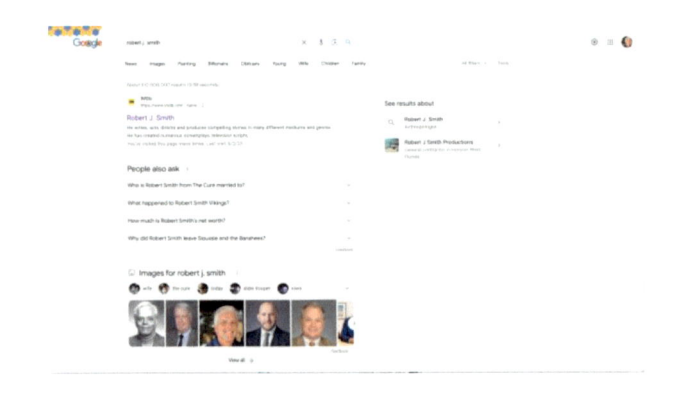

E.g., As of December 2023, there were 13,143,096 Internet Movie Database (IMDb) name rankings. Logic dictates that anyone who places in the *TOP* 131,431 of those name rankings, also places in the *TOP 1% on IMDb!* Verifiable statistics and measurements are your key to success. We have a simple and effective method that we utilize to qualify each and every one of our clients for IMDb profiles and all of their inherited *TOP of Google Search* rankings and benefits.

https://IMDb.Me/RobertJSmith

An IMDb "STARmeter" that ranks you in the *TOP 1%,* also helps with media relations, television bookings and even film opportunities. I've closed many contracts with this ranking alone. It's been all that several well-known corporations and other needed to see.

INFLUENCE IN ACTION™
GAINS PROVEN RESULTS AND DRIVES SALES

https://tinyurl.com/RJSPROonIMDB

You may use what you learn here to create your own plan of *ACTION* or you may easily book an appointment with me and allow me to guide you along your way to even greater success than you've already had.

https://SmithProfits.com/

It really is that simple. While almost nothing in business or in life that is worthwhile comes easy, we make many worthwhile opportunities simple. It's as easy as booking an appointment and as simple as implementing our proven strategies.

https://smithprofits.com/contact/

Chapter Five

Authority Marketing

Remember when I said, "It's impressive to see what kids can do, the very minute they upgrade their mindset to view their endless possibilities?" It's the same for you and me.

The *Affluent Homeowner* magazine that I published in place of a client newsletter, returned $53,000.00 with its very first use. The day after I mailed the first batch to clients I received a phone call. That call came from a client who was so ecstatic to receive her copy, that she called me right from her mailbox at the end of her long driveway to refer her 80-year-old friend to me. We made the appointment on the spot before we all realized that they were standing out in 96° heat and they could easily walk inside to enjoy their air conditioning and provide me with all of her necessary information.

INFLUENCE IN ACTION™
GAINS PROVEN RESULTS AND DRIVES SALES

Affluent Homeowner Magazine

Custom made persuasive sales and marketing pieces can be made to order regardless of your profession and industry. These methods are tried and true. There are many ways to gain authority through effective marketing: News Story Releases, Persuasive Comic Books, Books, Magazine Articles, and many more. It all comes down to a quick video call or phone call to determine which of these methods of *INFLUENCE IN ACTION*™ will *GAIN PROVEN RESULTS* for you and *DRIVE* more *SALES* to your business.

Authority marketing works as people learn from others and follow the leads of people who are experts in their fields. We should all strive to stand on the shoulders of giants. We know that authority marketing works because experts have been employing it for years. Does your competition employ authority marketing? If not, you will gain market share by employing this proven strategy. If they do, you will lose market share by failing to employ it.

Are you concerned that you lack authority and/or credibility? In the words of the Dr. Smith character in the 1960s television show, *LOST IN SPACE,* "Never fear, Smith is here!"

We can create instant authority for you with our proprietary news releases, written by your award-winning Master of Fine Arts Valedictorian and *Factual Storytelling*™ expert,

INFLUENCE IN ACTION™
GAINS PROVEN RESULTS AND DRIVES SALES

Yours Truly. Our news releases are GUARANTEED to be placed with major television networks and other well-known media outlets. Our financial advisory firm clients increased their sales closing rates 51% across the board with this single strategy in 2023. *What would a 51% increase in your income do for you in a single year?*

Chapter Six

Scarcity Marketing

One way to create legitimate scarcity is to be booked solid and stay booked solid. We provide clients with methods to create an endless supply of prospects and referrals. Another way to create legitimate scarcity is to obtain exclusive information and proprietary strategies and make them available to your prospects and clients alone. We provide this exclusive information, and these exclusive strategies to you, in order to drive record sales for you and your business.

How do you create legitimate scarcity when recruiting for positions and project opportunities? I recommended staying away from the "limited time only" language that most everyone uses, especially when the time is not truly limited.

On a book project opportunity, that I originally provided to team of ten co-authors, I began with authority marketing. As my previous co-author team and I reached #1 Bestseller rankings with *SALES GENIUS #1©* where we bested the "Wolf of Wall Street" whose book came in at #2. I was able to bring this screenshot to them to attract a few new co-authors.

While this strategy was effective, it was too slow for my liking. It was then that the Agatha Christie play *TEN LITTLE INDIANS* came to mind. I remembered viewing the film version, *AND THEN THERE WERE NONE* many years earlier. It was time to stand on the shoulders of a giant. I quickly developed what I call "The Christie Campaign." After all, who was better at building suspense than Agatha Christie who created this effective 'ticking clock' in story form?

INFLUENCE IN ACTION™
GAINS PROVEN RESULTS AND DRIVES SALES

With each successive co-author gained, I simply announced it on social media and noted how many opportunities were left. Of course, with each successive opportunity taken, there was one less available. It also helped that there are numerous movie posters, now in the public domain that are available to use.

Try this strategy with your next project or hiring event. If you have ten openings, start at the that number, if you have less openings, naturally start at the actual number of openings that you have. Here is a sample text, a parody text, if you like.

INFLUENCE IN ACTION™
GAINS PROVEN RESULTS AND DRIVES SALES

All that you have to do is customize it for your offering. If you have a need for more than ten, or if you need help in any way, just reach out to me at **https://SmithProfits.com/Contact** and we'll handle it for you inexpensively and effectively.

***AND THEN THERE WERE NONE*, Movie Poster**

Ten co-author spots went out to dine;
One was taken and then there were nine.

INFLUENCE IN ACTION™
GAINS PROVEN RESULTS AND DRIVES SALES

Nine co-author spots sat up very late;
Another was taken and then there were eight.

Eight co-author spots traveling in Devon;
A chapter was claimed, and then there were seven.

Seven co-author spots chopping up sticks;
Another chapter was gone, and then there were six.

Six co-author spots playing with a hive;
A fledgling author claimed one and then there were five.

Five co-author spots going in for law;
One needed no Chancery and then there were four.

Four co-author spots going out to sea;
A novice author claimed one and then there were three.

Three co-author spots walking in the zoo;

INFLUENCE IN ACTION™
GAINS PROVEN RESULTS AND DRIVES SALES

Another author claimed one and then there were two.

Two co-author spots sitting in the sun;
One got claimed up and then there was one.

One co-author spot left all alone;
It was claimed right up and then there were none.

Chapter Seven

Marketing with Consistency and Selling through Commitment

COMMITMENT – ALWAYS KEEP YOUR WORD.

Most of us have a strong desire to stay true to our word. When we make commitments, most of us strive to keep our word. It's human nature. In a perfect world, everyone would keep his or her word. The fact that some people don't only helps you to stand apart from the crowd. Keeping your word is not only a differentiator for you, it makes you distinctive.

This natural human desire to work with people who honor their commitments is a key to closing more sales and receiving more referrals than most people dare to dream of. We provide sales and service training, so that you achieve optimal success in both areas.

INFLUENCE IN ACTION™
GAINS PROVEN RESULTS AND DRIVES SALES

"Does the business have a consistent operating history?"- Warren Buffett

Consistency is obviously one of the things that the man considered to be the world's greatest investor looks for when evaluating companies to invest in. Since it's important to him, we are wise to make it important to us. Consistency is key in our work as well as it is in yours. We stay consistent with our industry rankings and our Google Search rankings with techniques that our firm has mastered. All of our methods are available to you. All at a small fraction of the cost of Google Ads and social media ads, and at a fraction of the cost of unnecessary paid SEO.

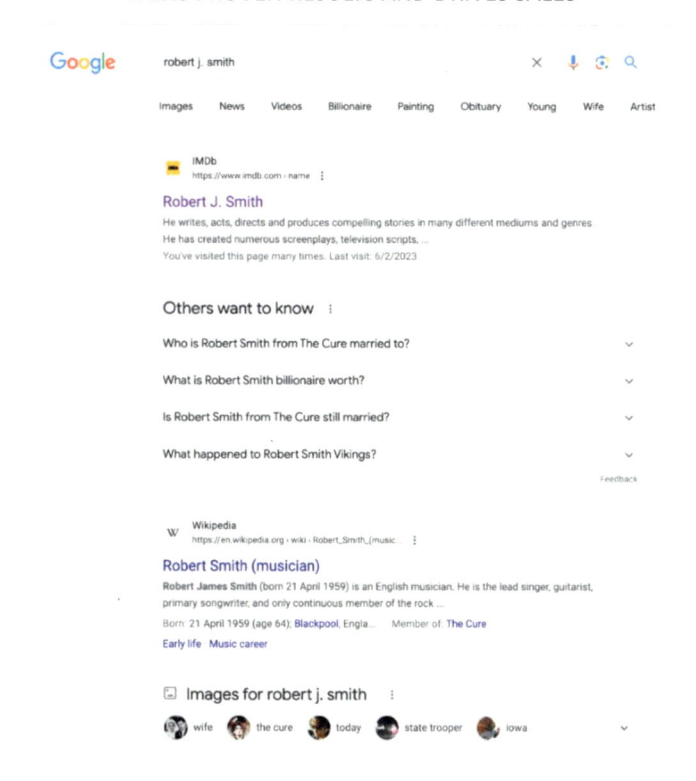

INFLUENCE IN ACTION™
GAINS PROVEN RESULTS AND DRIVES SALES

Consistency and our proprietary IMDb strategy keeps me ranked above a Rock & Roll Hall of Famer who has the same middle initial, a billionaire, and an NFL running back who became a network television football analyst.

    Of course, this happens when people search my name the way it is branded. When they search without our shared middle initial, the lead singer from The Cure wins. That's perfectly fine as that is not the way my businesses and I are branded.

Oddly enough, the rockstar is not the reason I brand my name with my middle initial. As our middle initials are identical that wouldn't make sense. The reason I branded my name that way is that there are four competing actors here in Florida alone, named Robert Smith.

I was cast in a film, drove across the state for the first day of shooting and discovered two of those other four actors there. As it turned out, the casting director was looking for me, and he mistakenly thought that the three separate E-mail addresses he found online while searching for me, were all mine.

It was at that moment I knew that I had to differentiate myself from my statewide namesakes. I had to make myself distinctive, and I immediately did. The best part was that as soon as I bought new domains and created new E-mail addresses, more film opportunities were presented to me and my IMDb "STARmeter" skyrocketed. The result? More opportunities to appear in television commercials including one on The Golf Channel, even though I haven't played golf in fifteen years, or even attended a PGA tournament in more than twenty years.

Why is that important to you? It's important because what I've been able to figure out on IMDb can help you or anyone gain *TOP of Google Search* rankings on the front page. We can do this for you at a fraction of the cost of whatever you may be doing now to improve your SEO and your search rankings.

We've had clients who were spending $10,000.00 per month in Google Ads to achieve front page rankings. Clients who are now saving that $120,000.00 per year. And, others who were spending $5,000.00 per month on SEO optimization who were able to scrap that and save $60,000.00 per year. What could you and your business do with an extra $60,000.00 - $120,000.00 to invest or spend each and every year?

Chapter Eight

Smile

People obviously prefer to do business with happy people that they do with people who are unhappy. People also do business with people they like and trust. Genuinely like your clients and they are more likely to do business with you, because they will like you as well.

There are many reasons for you and all of your employees to smile as often as possible. Those reasons are detailed in my Forbes article, *SMILE, YOU'RE ON BRANDED CAMERA!*

https://www.forbes.com/councils/forbesbusinesscouncil/2023/11/13/smile-youre-on-branded-camera-why-companies-should-include-smiles-in-their-branding/

Keep your smiles consistent in all of your branding, marketing, and sales.

We provide logo upgrades to take advantage of research that will make your brand more appealing to potential customers and clients. We also create mascots for clients with my team of MARVEL, DC Comics and Disney artists. Our Village Smithy has done wonders for us, as has our jingle that was created by one of our strategic partners:

https://tinyurl.com/RJSProJingle

Do what I've been doing for decades, "Have a Coke and a Smile!"

**Your Friendly Neighborhood Coke Man
Circa 1985**

It was as a young Coke Truck Driver where I learned the value of a smile. I always had a friendly smile and a firm handshake for everyone I delivered my product to. As a result, I outsold every other deliveryman around. I did this for the two years I was there.

I also learned quickly that a genuine smile helps us in our personal lives as well as it helps us in our business lives. While my co-workers often struggled to find dates, I never had a problem finding them, as they most often found me. This is really no secret. People generally want to be with people who are in a good mood.

For example, as a young man, when my co-workers, my friends, and I went out at night, they would often walk into a nightclub or a concert trying to look tough or cool. In short, many of them were posers. This strategy, of course, was ineffective. Contrary to all of that, I would walk in, already having a good time, and expecting to continue to have good time. The result, I never lacked a dance partner.

If you ever find yourself struggling to succeed, or just to make friends, simply try to be happy. See if that works for you. I'm willing to bet on you and bet that this decades-long strategy will work for you as well as it has for me!

When you smile, you'll enjoy yourself more and your business will see increased profits. When all of this happens, you won't be able to keep from smiling!

Ask yourself, "How much does it cost to smile?"

Get happy and try your smile on for size. See what it does for you.

Here is an article that I wrote in Forbes magazine that illustrates just what a smile has done for some of the world's largest companies:

Smile, You're On Branded Camera: Why Companies Should Include Smiles In Their Branding

The Internet Movie Database (IMDb) logline for the hit television show, Candid

Camera is, "Unsuspecting people are placed in confusing, impossible, embarrassing, ridiculous, and hilarious positions, while their reactions are recorded on a hidden camera."

There is no doubt that companies that fail to brand their products and services effectively will also find themselves in "confusing, impossible, embarrassing, ridiculous, and hilarious positions." Brands tell stories. Do you want the story of your business to be a sad one or a happy one? Put a smile on your customers' faces and you'll put a smile on your own face.

My brother, Ron, learned this long ago. In fact, as a painter, he begins every job by painting a smile in a prominent place that eventually gets painted over. Nevertheless, that's Ron's trademark, and that smile will last as long as each particular building does. Not only that but also Ron provides every customer with what he terms his "All Smiles Guarantee." Ron's smile tells the story of his business. His customers know they can expect to have a happy experience with Ron and his crew members. They know this from referrals and Ron's reputation. They all come together to tell the story of the painting business.

What's your business story? The first part of your story that potential customers see is your company logo. I believe this is why so many successful companies place smiles in their logos. Here are some well-known examples of brands that use imagery representative of smiles:

- Colgate's branding makes the most sense, as it promotes its products as solutions to more beautiful smiles.
- Amazon may be the most famous logo with a smile on it.
- Dannon/Danone gave its health-focused foods a logo boost to help people smile.
- Kraft Mac & Cheese took things a step further and turned a macaroni noodle into a smile.

We were so impressed with the statistics on providing subliminal smiles in branding that we upgraded our RobertJSmith.com, Smith Profits, Robert J.

Smith Productions and Smith Comics logos with upward curves that represent smiles as well.

Lay's took smiles seriously in a campaign called "The Smile Stories" to help make lives better. Here is an excerpt from the Now This website: "Lay's is celebrating people across the country who inspire smiles in their communities in extraordinary ways ... Each Smile with Lay's bag you buy helps us reach our goal of a $1 million donation to Operation Smile – a nonprofit that changes and saves lives one smile at a time."

Operation Smile takes smiles seriously as well. However, smiles are not a for-profit business for Operation Smile as it is for Frito-Lay and Colgate. Operation Smile operates as a not-for-profit 501(c)(3) organization that provides life-improving cleft surgery, dentistry, orthodontics, speech therapy and psychological services. This organization makes me think of a young girl named Veda Roznowski, who this article is dedicated to. She passed away at the tender age of one due to complications from anesthesia at a local hospital during a surgery Operation Smile specializes in.

"Let us always meet each other with a smile, for the smile is the beginning of love," Mother Teresa is known to have said.

The world's largest companies have leveraged the emotions of happiness and love in their branding and advertising campaigns to elicit feelings of unity which greatly influence our buying decisions.

"Have a Coke and a Smile" is one example. The world's largest soft drink manufacturer had great success with its campaign of togetherness and symmetry, which culminated in the huge success of its Mean Joe Greene Super Bowl ad that featured his fictional meeting with a young fan.

Even the word "smile" can sell without anyone actually seeing a smiling face. Dean Martin, Doris Day, and many others sold a massive number of records with the song "Powder Your Face with Sunshine," the lyrics say, "Put on a great big smile. Make up your eyes with laughter. Folks will be laughing with you in a little while. Whistle a tune of gladness. Blue never was in style. The future's brighter when hearts are lighter. So, smile, smile, smile."

Dozens of artists sold records with the song "When You're Smiling," which was first published in 1928. "When you're smiling, when you're smiling, the whole world smiles with you," the lyrics say. "When you're laughing, when you're laughing, the sun comes shining through. But when you're crying, you bring on the rain. So, stop your sighing, be happy again. Keep on smiling, 'cause when you're smiling, the whole world smiles with you."

Of course, *Smile* was the album the Beach Boys abandoned in 1967.

When Brian Wilson resurrected the album, *Smile in 2004,* he earned his first Grammy with one of its tracks, and *Brian Wilson Presents Smile* reached No. 13 in the U.S. and No. 7 in the UK (paywall). *BWPS* also landed in Rolling stone's "500 Greatest Albums Of All Time."

INFLUENCE IN ACTION™
GAINS PROVEN RESULTS AND DRIVES SALES

"A smile is the best makeup any girl can wear," Marilyn Monroe is famously attributed with saying.

Here's the best news: Research has shown that you don't even need an obvious, full-blown smile. An upward curve does the trick. We've updated our logos at Smith Profits with upward curves across the board, and we're having a record fourth quarter as a result.

A combined research study in Colombia and the United Kingdom said that "these findings provide both a deeper theoretical understanding of the influence of subtle cues on evaluation and decision making, and concrete, practical information for both product designers and marketers."[1]

Don't fail to brand your company's products and services effectively and find yourself in "confusing, impossible, embarrassing, ridiculous, and hilarious

---

[1] Smiles over Frowns: When Curved Lines Influence Product Preference, July 2015, Psychology and Marketing. Alejandro Salgado-Montejo, Isabel Tapia León, Andrew J. Elliot, and Carlos Jose Salgado.

positions." Instead, brand your products and services effectively, and you'll always smile, whether you are on camera or not.

Chapter Nine

Customer/Client Conformity and Referrals

People like to see what others do before making decisions. In short, the vast majority of people commonly conform to what others are doing. In its simplest form, "Monkey see, monkey do." Most people don't want to take the time necessary to make sound decisions for themselves. It's more efficient to "follow the leader." For most people, there is "Safety in Numbers" and they don't see much risk in doing as others do.

This is not only true when it comes to making buying decisions, it's true in social situations as well. When mentoring a high school Entrepreneur Pitch Competitor, several of us agreed to serve as her "Advisory Board" to lend credibility and authority to her and the medical device that she was "pitching."

INFLUENCE IN ACTION™
GAINS PROVEN RESULTS AND DRIVES SALES

MEET OUR ADVISORY BOARD

Kevin Harrington — Original Shark from Shark Tank Marketing Advisory

Dr. Erik Rauch — Platinum Award Winning Medical/USF Nurse Anesthesiology Program

Dr. Robert J. Smith — Writer/Forbes magazine Financial Advisor

Loc Hoang — Engineering professional Engineering/Construction of Product Advisory

As soon as this slide appeared, roughly half of the crowd immediately stood to give her an ovation within seconds, others followed, and very quickly, everyone who could stand was standing and clapping. This was conformity *IN ACTION*.

We can help you to understand the advantages and disadvantages of public conformity and help you *DRIVE SALES*. We can also help you drive referrals to your business with a system of expectation and conformity. A proven referral system is crucial to your business as it all but eliminates your cost of acquiring a news customer or client.

We have a proven strategy to obtain stellar recommendations and reviews for your business while providing Google Business Profile Updates targeting "ready to buy" customers. We provide exclusive access to well-known business authorities for endorsements. We've also got a brand new strategy to help you land in searches when searches aren't necessarily looking for you and your business. This proven tech strategy is so brand new, that we haven't even had time to bring it to all of our existing clients yet!

Chapter Ten

Marketing through Affiliation

Merriam-Webster defines Affiliation as "the state of having shared interests or efforts (as in social or business matters)."

Here is a proven method to gain new clients by way of referrals and affiliation marketing: Years ago, when I was working for John Hancock in metro Detroit, I had a client who is an OB/GYN named Sidney Smith. Dr. Smith used to invite me to his monthly medical society meetings to meet his fellow surgeons.

Sidney used to tell me that he liked to brag to them about what a great job his "financial man" was doing for him. Dr. Smith has a great sense of humor. As he is black and I am white, he used to introduce me as his brother. When his fellow surgeons gave a double-take, and they always did, he would say, "It's okay. I'm the black sheep of the family."

INFLUENCE IN ACTION™

GAINS PROVEN RESULTS AND DRIVES SALES

That line always drew a laugh, and it always did something wonderful. It brought the natural defenses of his fellow surgeons down and made them more receptive to my message.

Dr. Smith is a brilliant marketer. One evening, at his country club, where these meetings are held, he pulled me aside with drink in hand and said, "You know, I'm tired of introducing you as Mr. Smith to Dr. So, and So. You see, many of these guys think they are better than they really are and they think that being doctors, they are somehow better than everyone else."

He looked me in the eye and asked "How about you level the playing field for me and earn a doctorate degree so that I can introduce you as Dr. Smith to Dr. So, and So?" And that, Wise Reader, was the impetus for earning my Ph.D. in business.

While earning a doctorate was helpful in working with surgeons, no doctoral degree is necessary to become wildly effective when marketing to groups of people who have an

INFLUENCE IN ACTION™
GAINS PROVEN RESULTS AND DRIVES SALES

affinity for one another. Naturally, provide useful products and services to them, and develop systems for gaining referrals and repeat business.

To *GAIN PROVEN RESULTS, DRIVE SALES* and increase profits, add these three things to what you've learned so far:

1. Understand affiliate marketing.
2. Level the playing field...and tilt it in your favor when you can.
3. Play the percentages.

Chapter Eleven

Playing the Percentages

This book is your key to improved performance and results. This chapter is your roadmap to #1 worldwide rankings, *provided you put this plan to work for you and you take CONSISTENT ETHICAL ACTIONS IN ORDER TO SUCCEED WITH IT!*

As Paul Harvey famously said, "And now, the rest of the story…" The ability to influence others comes only from an understanding of human nature. None of these strategies are effective with 100% of the people, 100% of the time. No principle, strategy, or technique ever is. The key to success is to utilize these persuasive strategies the way a successful baseball manager "plays the percentages." No person, business or baseball manager ever wins 100% of the time. However, when we play the percentages, we win more times than we lose. The reverse is true when we fail to play the percentages.

INFLUENCE IN ACTION™
GAINS PROVEN RESULTS AND DRIVES SALES

Case Study: The 1984 World Series between my beloved Detroit Tigers and the San Diego Padres.

Here is an example of a manager who failed to play the percentages. In doing so, Padres manager, Dick Williams allowed his team's season to come to an end. He let his team down, his team's fans down and he let himself down. With runners on second and third with one out and first base open, the percentage play was to walk Kirk Gibson to set up a double play.

Being a Tigers fan, this is my favorite MLB moment of all-time. As Williams walks to the mound to talk to pitcher, Goose Gossage, Tigers manager Sparky Anderson says to Roger Craig "If he changes his mind, I don't believe it. (I'll) never believe it as long as I live." Anderson turns his attention to Gibson at the plate. "He doesn't wanna walk you! He doesn't wanna walk you!" {sic} Anderson motions to Gibson to swing away.

Sure enough, Gossage talks Williams out of walking Gibson. Anderson has the smile of a man who knows what happens when the opposition fails to play the percentages. Two pitches later, announcer Vin Scully exclaims "And there it goes!" Gibson homers into the upper deck at Tiger Stadium, scoring three runs and effectively closes out the series. Announcer, Joe Garagiola, "And that'll be one of those things that'll haunt Dick Williams."

Scully paraphrases the poet, Whittier, "Saddest words of tongue and pen…what might have been, for San Diego…Here's the story of the inning, of the game, of the series, of the year! "

https://SmithProfits.com

Don't let the "saddest of words…what might have been" haunt you for the rest of your life. Take **ACTION** now. Learn these proven strategies, employ *Factual Storytelling* ™ into your business or career, and you cannot fail.

INFLUENCE IN ACTION™
GAINS PROVEN RESULTS AND DRIVES SALES

**Lifelong Detroit Tigers Fans,
Sharon and Your Author**

You've seen how you can reach *the TOP of PAGE ONE in Name Brand and Company Brand Google Searches*.

You've seen how the proper, *ETHICAL ACTIONS* can elevate you to *TOP 1% and #1 WORLWIDE RANKINGS IN YOUR INDUSTRY!*

Use this roadmap or easily contact me to be your guide.

Climb aboard! When we stand on the shoulders of giants, there is plenty of room for everyone! You have an abundance of opportunities before you and ahead of you! Now is your time to claim those opportunities.

The difference in your success and that if your competitors, is the *ACTION* you take versus the *ACTIONS* they don't take. People like you read about these proven methods, take *ACTION*, and grow your businesses, revenues, and profits, while others will only read about them.

Put these *PROVEN* strategies into *ACTION!* Click on this QR code now, to experience fast and efficient RESULTS on your way to the TOP of your industry!

Robert@RobertJSmith.com | +1 **(407) 508-0200** | https://calendly.com/RJSPRO/book

Epilogue

Now that you've read though *INFLUENCE IN ACTION*™ *GAINS PROVEN RESULTS AND DRIVES SALES* what *ACTIONS* are you taking?

Are you bringing Factual Storytelling™ into your business for fast and effective results?

Are you successfully influencing people in business and in your personal life?

Like an accomplished boxer, will you also use your awareness *of* influence strategies to defend yourself against the unethical actions of others?

Hopefully, you will take the time now to create a list of *ACTION* items that you will take immediately to improve your business, career or other circumstances. And hopefully, the answer to all of the remaining questions is a resounding "YES!"

Take reciprocation for example. I interviewed the late great Eddie Money for a couple of magazines that I wrote for. He was kind enough to provide me with an audio plug without my even asking for it. "I want to thank you for the publicity you are bringing to the Pediatric AIDS Foundation and to the Intrepid Fallen Heroes Fund. From what I understand, you have a pretty prominent career in this business, and you have a lot of respect. I appreciate the fact that we had the opportunity to visit and do this interview."

Celebrating Two Tickets to Paradise with Sharon and the Late, Great, Eddie Money

He was also kind enough to always have backstage passes waiting for Sharon and me to bring our daughter, Sabrina to see him and his band every time they came to Orlando or Tampa Bay. He also provided Sabrina with her first opportunity to be in the press pit and capture photos of his show while she was still in high school. Sabrina did so well that we were later able to get her into the press pit for Alice Cooper where she did a tremendous job and was able to network with other professional photographers at iHeart Radio and other media outlets.

While Webster's Dictionary defines the word *Reciprocate* as to "to return in kind or degree," and most people do, it is important to note that not everyone does.

This is why it is always best to give with no anticipation of receiving anything in return. When people *Reciprocate* in kind, as most do, it's a bonus. When they fail to *Reciprocate* in kind, nothing is lost.

INFLUENCE IN ACTION™
GAINS PROVEN RESULTS AND DRIVES SALES

"Action is the foundational key to all success."
– Pablo Picasso

No matter what you decide to do after reading INFLUENCE IN ACTION™ GAINS PROVEN RESULTS AND DRIVES SALES, you are now fully equipped to take ACTION in your own business or career. You also have all of the support you that you will ever need to GAIN PROVEN RESULTS OF YOUR OWN.

All of our very best to you, your family, and your business!

INFLUENCE IN ACTION™
GAINS PROVEN RESULTS AND DRIVES SALES

About Your Author

ROBERT J. SMITH, MFA

Born in metro Detroit, Smith learned to compete at a young age, winning baseball championships in his first season at the age of nine and in his final season at the age of thirty, including s streak of six out of his first eight seasons, all on eight different teams.

His work ethic was developed in his blue-collar beginnings. No one in the history of Automobile Capital of the World, or in the Great State of Michigan, has completed more oil changes in one day, one week, or one month than Smith has. In fact, he averaged two cars at once from 6:30 a.m. to midnight, seven days per week, for thirty-one straight days during a Mobil Oil recall in the early 1980s.

After moving to Florida, Smith and another route driver teamed up to complete all of their deliveries after every other route truck driver for Coca-Cola was called back into the warehouse during Hurricane Elena. After developing the #1 home market merchandising route in the Sarasota territory, Smith suffered an on-the-job injury which led to a career change into the financial services industry.

As a financial services advisor, Smith reached #1 worldwide rankings at AXA Financial, The Equitable, Mutual of New York (MONY), and BankAtlantic/BB&T/SunTrust/Truist. He set records at John Hancock and New York Life. His name is enshrined in a plaque on Madison Avenue.

INFLUENCE IN ACTION™
GAINS PROVEN RESULTS AND DRIVES SALES

https://smithprofits.com/

Debilitating spine and other severe injuries necessitated a career change. While undergoing multiple surgeries to regain the ability to walk, he concurrently earned his Master of Fine Arts (MFA) in Creative Writing as Valedictorian at Full Sail University, and his Feature Film Writing degree "With Distinction" at UCLA. He holds Director's Awards for "The Art of Visual Storytelling" as well as "Editing for Film, Games and Animation."

http://www.RobertJSmith.com

Smith's consulting practice helps financial advisors reach the TOP 1% in production, entertainers reach the TOP 1% of Internet Movie Database (IMDb), and every client gain TOP of Google Search Rankings.

http://www.RobertJSmithProductions.com

He is an International Best-Selling Author with **SALES GENIUS #1©,** which bested The Wolf of Wall Street's book on sales. **THE ADVENTURES OF INSURANCEMAN©** increases sales for clients and their companies. Smith created **SHORT ATTENTION SPAN DAN**© to teach writing and public speaking to students.

Robert J. Smith, MFA's Amazon Author Page

After earning his Leadership Certification in Influencing People at the University of Michigan, Smith earned Certification with Maxwell Leadership and has turned dozens of businesspeople into #1 International Bestselling Authors.

Smith and his companies have been featured on ABC, CBS, CW, FOX, The Golf Channel, NBC, WGN, and hundreds of other media outlets.

http://www.IMDb.Me/RobertJSmith

He's been named to the Entrepreneur Magazine Leadership Network and, as a member of the Forbes Business Council contributed monthly articles to the magazine.

https://www.forbes.com/councils/forbesbus

inesscouncil/people/smittyrobertjsmith/

Smith's other book titles in the works include, **#1: HOW TO REACH THE VERY TOP IN YOUR INDUSTRY – NO MATTER YOUR PROFESSION, EVERYTHING YOU ALWAYS WANTED TO ABOUT INCREASING BUSINESS**AND WERE AFRAID TO ASK, INFLUENCE IN ACTION BRINGS MORE BUSINESS TO ENTREPRENEURS**, and many others.

https://SmithProfits.com/Books/

Smith raised millions for charity and volunteers in public and private schools. Within 24-hours in 2024, one of his high school students, and one of his medical school students each won their Entrepreneur Pitch Championships and earned sizable cash prizes to develop each of their medical products that will greatly benefit mankind.

He's served as a Field Councilman for the Greater Detroit Area Life Underwriters, Board Member of the Tampa Bay United Way,

Treasurer of World League Baseball, and President of the Executive Sports Council.

He lives in Winter Garden, Florida, with Sharon Roznowski and has three children: Ashley, Austin, and Sabrina.

INFLUENCE IN ACTION™
GAINS PROVEN RESULTS AND DRIVES SALES

Coming Soon

INFLUENCE IN ACTION™
BRINGS MORE BUSINESS TO ENTREPRENEURS©

#1 INTERNATIONAL BEST SELLER

Successful Actions Based on Five Decades of Success with Several of the World's Largest Corporations and Companies Like Yours!

FOREWORD BY **SHARON L. ROZNOWSKI, M.ED.**

INFLUENCE IN ACTION™
BRINGS MORE BUSINESS TO ENTREPRENUERS

ROBERT J. SMITH, MFA

WITH CHAPTERS BY,
ANISH VERMA AND
LEELAN RODRIGUEZ

INFLUENCE IN ACTION™
GAINS PROVEN RESULTS AND DRIVES SALES

INFLUENCE IN ACTION™
TO EDUCATE STUDENTS©

INFLUENCE IN ACTION™
GAINS PROVEN RESULTS AND DRIVES SALES

INFLUENCE IN ACTION™
FOR AUTOMOTIVE PROFESSIONALS©

#1 BEST SELLING SERIES

Four Decades of Success with the Big Three and Others

INFLUENCE IN *ACTION*™
for AUTOMOTIVE PROFESSIONALS

ROBERT J. SMITH, MFA and
Automotive Experts

INFLUENCE IN ACTION™
GAINS PROVEN RESULTS AND DRIVES SALES

INFLUENCE IN ACTION™ *FOR SALES PROFESSIONALS*©

(Cover Coming Soon)

INFLUENCE IN ACTION™
GAINS PROVEN RESULTS AND DRIVES SALES

EVERYTHING YOU ALWAYS WANTED TO KNOW ABOUT INCREASING BUSINESS*

*AND WERE AFRAID TO ASK

EXPLAINED BY ROBERT J. SMITH, MFA AND HIS FORBES ARTICLES©

Everything you always wanted to know about increasing business*

*AND WERE AFRAID TO ASK

Explained by
Robert J. Smith, MFA
and his Forbes articles

INFLUENCE IN ACTION™
GAINS PROVEN RESULTS AND DRIVES SALES

#1
HOW TO REACH THE TOP IN YOUR INDUSTRY NO MATTER YOUR PROFESSION©

(Cover Coming Soon)
And

Our most ambitious project to-date:

WHAT AMERICA MEANS TO ME©

A revolutionary new book series where we will help 1,000 students and teachers, plus administrative and support staff to become #1 Best Selling Authors!

To become involved and support this project, please feel free to reach out to me direct at (407) 508-0200 and/or
Robert@RobertJSmith.com

Thank you.

INFLUENCE IN ACTION™
GAINS PROVEN RESULTS AND DRIVES SALES

Coming Soon from
SMITH COMICS:

THE ADVENTURES OF INSURANCEWOMAN©

REAL ESTATE WOMAN©

REAL ESTATE MAN©

THE AMAZING WEBSITE-MAN©

THE LOAN ARRANGER©

SUPER DENTIST©

SHERRY MASON©

THE ADVENTURES OF BERNIE BURNS©

SHORT ATTENTION SPAN DAN:
THE GREAT HOUDAN©

SHORT ATTENTION SPAN DAN:
WILD THING, YOU MOVE ME©

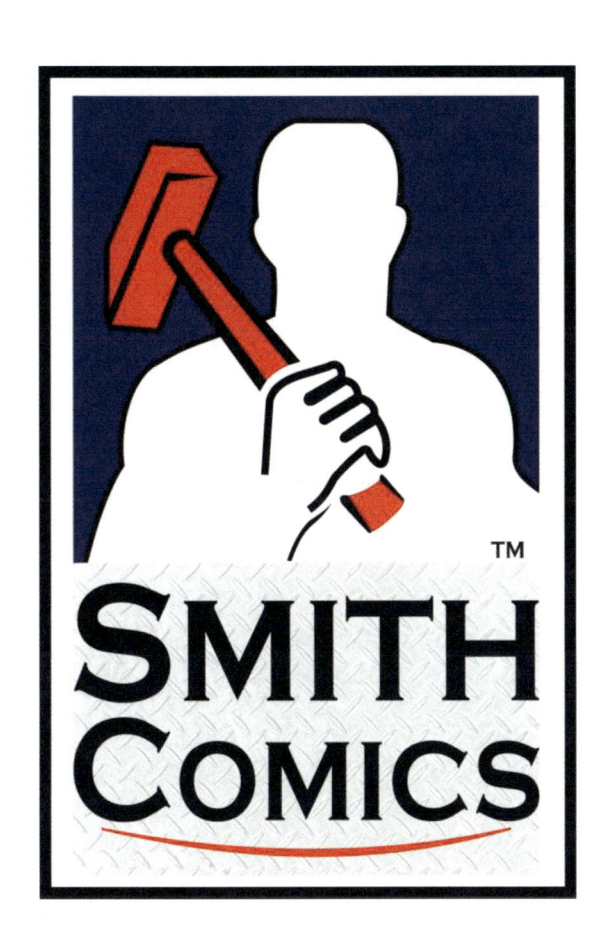

INFLUENCE IN ACTION™
GAINS PROVEN RESULTS AND DRIVES SALES

INFLUENCE IN ACTION™
GAINS PROVEN RESULTS AND DRIVES SALES

Wise Reader, this is your opportunity to transform yourself into a Wise Doer.

Take *ACTION* to *GAIN PROVEN RESULTS AND DRIVE SALES* for your business.

Book your no cost, initial consultation now at:

https://SmithProfits.com/Contact

Learn how you can eliminate your business problems and optimize all of your opportunities.

https://SmithProfits.com

INFLUENCE IN ACTION™
GAINS PROVEN RESULTS AND DRIVES SALES

"Well done is better than well said."
-Benjamin Franklin

INFLUENCE IN ACTION™
GAINS PROVEN RESULTS AND DRIVES SALES

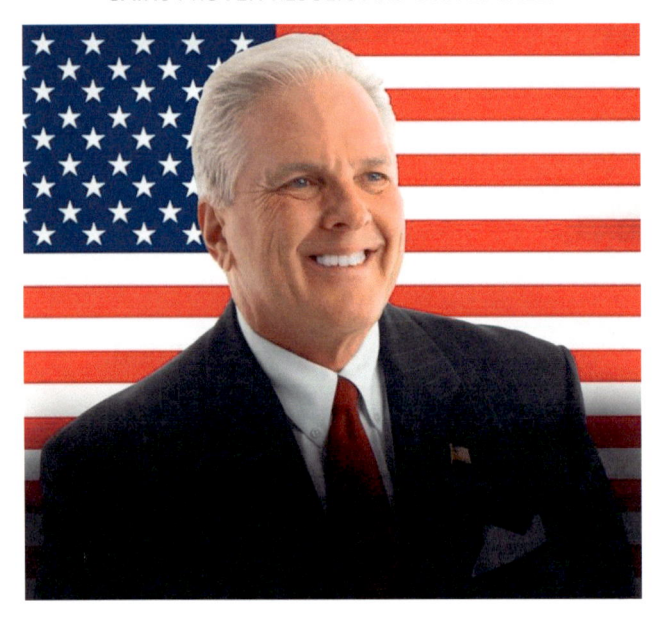

Made in the USA
Columbia, SC
10 January 2025

776d5731-98bc-411c-bb1b-d1364e543908R01